W9-AAF-721

INVESTIGATE BIODIVERSITY

FISH

Enslow Publishing
101 W. 23rd Street
Suite 240
New York, NY 10011
USA
enslow.com

Heather Moore Niver

●●● Words to Know

anadromous Traveling from the sea to freshwater to lay eggs.

aquarium A tank where fish live.

cartilage A strong but flexible substance.

gills Organs that remove oxygen from water.

larva An early type of baby that usually doesn't look like its parents yet.

oxygen A gas that plants and animals need in order to live.

predator An animal that hunts another animal for food.

prey Animals that are hunted by others for food.

scales Small, flat plates that cover a fish.

species Kinds of animals

vertebrates Group of animals that have a backbone.

Contents

Finned Friends

Fish are fun! Maybe you or someone you know has fish in a tank. Or you've seen them in a zoo or **aquarium**. They can be a simple orange goldfish in a bowl or a seahorse. There are more than 22,000 different **species**, or kinds, of fish swimming around today.

Fish are **vertebrates**. This means they have a backbone. And of course they live in the water. Fish breathe underwater with organs called **gills**. Most fish have a smooth body. They are covered with **scales**. Fish are cold blooded. Their body temperature changes with their surroundings.

Kinds of Fish

There are three basic kinds of fish. They are bony, cartilaginous, and jawless. Each of these three kinds of fish has a different body. Let's learn about each type.

A pair of angelfish swim near a coral reef.

Bony Fish

Bony fish have a skeleton made of bone. On the outside, they have layers of thin scales. These scales make a smooth surface. It's perfect for gliding through the water. Ninety-five percent of all fish are bony fish. Some examples of bony fish are eels, seahorses, puffer fish, and mudskippers.

A puffer fish puffs up
when it senses danger.

6

A tiger shark gets its name from the dark stripes along its side.

Cartilaginous Fish

Cartilaginous fish hardly have bones at all! Only their teeth and scales are bone. Their bodies are mainly made of bendable **cartilage**. This is a substance in the body that is strong and flexible. And their scales are rooted right in their skin. Fish in this group include sharks, dogfish, rays, and skates.

Fast Fact

Fish have been swimming
around in the earth's waters for
450 million years!

Jawless Fish

Jawless fish have bony skeletons. But, as their name shows, they do not have a jaw. Instead, they have big mouths that suck. Other fish have pairs of fins, but jawless fish do not. Lampreys and hagfish are the only jawless fish around today. Lampreys suck the blood of other fish. Hagfish dine on dead fish.

Fish Life

● ● ● Fish swim by moving their tail fins back and forth. Their fins help them steer, balance, and stop. Only the seahorse swims in an upright position. Fish have a neat trick if they need to move in a hurry.

Fish use their tail fins to move along in the water.

They blow water out of their gills! The force of the water makes them dart forward.

Fish Food

Most fish make their meals of other fish. They also snack on invertebrates, or animals that do not have backbones. This **prey** is often swallowed whole. The smallest fish eat small plants.

The growth from the anglerfish's head attracts its prey. When prey gets close, the anglerfish gobbles it up.

Fish that get their meals off the seabed have mouths that open downward. Fish that munch on meals from the water's surface have mouths that open upward.

The Anglerfish has its own fishing rod. It hangs over its head and in front of its mouth. Anglerfish that live in the deep sea have glowing bait.

Fast Fact

The smallest fish are gobies. They can be less than half an inch (13 millimeters) long. The largest is the whale shark. These beasts can be 50 feet (15 meters) long and weigh 20 tons!

Fish like these perch travel in schools to stay safe.

Fish like to hang out in groups. These are called schools. Schools are safe places for fish. They are protected from **predators**. What happens if a school of fish is attacked? The school may stretch out in a line. Sometimes they split into groups of two. Then they swim in different directions.

In schools, the group finds food together. Every fish is better fed. It is also easier for fish to find a mate as part of a school.

Hey, Babies!

Most fish are hatched from eggs. A female lays her eggs in the water. The eggs grow outside her body. Eggs and babies may be eaten by other fish. Fish have interesting ways of protecting their eggs. The mother lays as many as a million eggs at a time! Some fish build a nest in the sand.

Fish Fathers

Male fish help take care of eggs and babies. The male seahorse carries the babies in a special pouch. Catfish males carry eggs in their mouths! They cannot eat until the eggs hatch. These dads may go a month without eating.

A group of fish eggs. Fish may lay many eggs, but they do not all survive.

These male seahorses are carrying eggs in their pouches. Some carry over a thousand eggs at a time!

Stickleback fathers build the mother a special tube. She lays her eggs inside. Then the male is in charge of the eggs. He chases the female away and guards the eggs. If an egg falls out, he puts it right back in the nest. He even takes care of the babies once they hatch. Baby fish are called fry.

It's Alive!

Some female fish keep the eggs in their bodies until they hatch. The babies hatch inside her. These eggs are called **larvae**. Some fish give birth to live babies. Sharks and guppies are two examples.

Fast Fact

Goldfish do not have eyelids. They don't blink! And they sleep with their eyes open.

A newly hatched tuna larva. A few eggs are nearby, waiting to hatch.

Some fish travel to specific places to lay their eggs. Salmon live at sea. But they lay eggs in freshwater. They are called **anadromous**. Some fish do the opposite. They live in freshwater. Then they lay their eggs in salt water.

Water, Water Everywhere

Fish live in all kinds of water. Seventy percent of the planet is covered with water. Some fish live in ponds. Others live in raging river waters. Some live in freezing cold water. Some live in hot springs. And still others live in salty ocean water.

Vertebrates need **oxygen** to live. That means fish do, too. Most fish have gills to get oxygen from the water. Bony fish use their mouths to take in water. Cartilaginous fish have special skin flaps. As water moves over the gills, they take in oxygen. Water is forced out and over the gills as the fish opens and closes its mouth.

Tricky Fish

Fish have lots of enemies. They have some tricks to keep from becoming another fish's next meal. For example, some fish have spots near their tails. Another fish might think this is

A whale shark's gills allow it to take in oxygen.

Can you spot the fish? This stonefish can make itself blend into the ocean floor.

their head. They attack the tail and the fish has a chance to swim away to safety. Other fish have a special talent. They can change color. Some can even change their colors into patterns. They match the area around them. This helps them hide from other fish.

Fish are a source of food for humans. Others enjoy keeping them as pets. A lot of our water has been hurt by pollution. We need to keep the water clean so fish will swim there happily for many more years.

Fast Fact

Fish cannot live in super salty water. For example, no fish live in the Great Salt Lake in Utah.

Activity: Class Pet

● ● ● With the help of a parent or teacher, get a fish as a class pet. Check books or the internet to figure out the kind of fish you want. What does the fish need to survive? Things to think about are:

- What does it eat?
- How often does it eat?
- What temperature water does it need?
- Does it get along with other fish?

Your research will help you think of other things your fish needs.

If you cannot get a fish as a pet, you can still do some research. Pick the kind of fish you might like to have. Do research to find out what you would need to care for your fish.

●●● Learn More

Books

Jacobson, Bray. *Fish Life Cycles*. New York, NY: Gareth Stevens, 2018.

Martin, Bobi. *What Are Fish?* New York, NY: Britannica Educational Publishing, 2017.

Niver, Heather Moore. *20 Fun Facts About Anglerfish*. New York, NY: Gareth Stevens, 2013.

Websites

Ducksters

www.ducksters.com/animals/fish.php

Fun fish facts with links to information about specific kinds of fish.

National Geographic Kids

kids.nationalgeographic.com/animals/hubs/fish

Learn about all different kinds of fish with photos.

●●● Index

Published in 2019 by Enslow Publishing, LLC.
101 W. 23rd Street, Suite 240, New York, NY 10011

Copyright © 2019 by Enslow Publishing, LLC.
All rights reserved.

No part of this book may be reproduced by any means without the written permission of the publisher.

Library of Congress Cataloging-in-Publication Data
Names: Niver, Heather Moore, author.
Title: Fish / Heather Moore Niver.
Description: New York : Enslow Publishing, 2019. | Series: Investigate biodiversity | Audience: Grade K-4. | Includes bibliographical references and index.
Identifiers: LCCN 2018010351| ISBN 9781978501867 (library bound) | ISBN 9781978502444 (paperback) | ISBN 9781978502451 (6 pack)
Subjects: LCSH: Fishes—Juvenile literature.
Classification: LCC QL617.2 .N58 2019 | DDC 597—dc23
LC record available at https://lccn.loc.gov/2018010351

Printed in the United States of America

To Our Readers: We have done our best to make sure all website addresses in this book were active and appropriate when we went to press. However, the author and the publisher have no control over and assume no liability for the material available on those websites or on any websites they may link to. Any comments or suggestions can be sent by e-mail to customerservice@enslow.com.

Photo Credits: Cover, p. 1 Rostislav Glinsky /Shutterstock.com; pp. 3, 14 Andrey Nekrasov/Getty Images; pp. 3, 6 ronnisantoso/RooM/ Getty Images; pp. 3, 19 Baptiste Severine/EyeEm/ Getty Images; pp. 3, 5 Vlad61 /Shutterstock.com; pp. 3, 23 Elizaveta Galitckaia / Shutterstock.com; p. 7 le bouil baptiste/ Shutterstock.com; p. 9 MattiaATH/Shutterstock.com; p. 10 David Shale/Nature Picture Library/Getty Images; p. 12 aquapix/Shutterstock.com; p. 15 Clive Bromhall/Oxford Scientic/Getty Images; p. 17 Gavin Parsons/Oxford Scientic/Getty Images; p. 20 Andrea Izzotti/Shutterstock.com; cover graphics magic pictures/Shutterstock.com.